K Y L I E

THE OFFICIAL 1991 ANNUAL

Published in Great Britain by World International Publishing Ltd.,
an Egmont Company, Egmont House,
P.O.Box 111, Great Ducie Street, Manchester M60 3BL.
Printed in Italy. ISBN 0 7235 6896 0
1st Reprint

£4.25

CONTENTS

A new decade - and an important new year for Kylie Minogue.

1990 marked the fourth year of Kylie's phenomenal success story. Could she maintain her popularity and acclaim? Could she still be the star everyone talked about and photographed? Could Kylie stay on top?

INTO TH

The answer is yes, yes and yes!

The past year has provided Kylie with some of the happiest and most rewarding moments of her career. As one critic said, Kylie must have the Midas touch.

The major highlights of the past year include her second album "Enjoy Yourself", the release of her first film "The Delinquents" and her first concert tours of Australia, the UK and Europe.

Kylie has taken a firm hold on all aspects of her career. She's taking an active part in the concept for her videos, she works closely with her band and dancers in the staging of her concerts and she's more aware of making the right career and business moves.

On a personal note, the shy girl-next-door has blossomed to a stylish, independent and confident woman, ready to take on the Nineties. Kylie celebrated her 22nd birthday on May 28.

These days there's no doubt she is more at ease with herself and the world around her. Kylie is taking a great interest in the environment and learning what she can do to help and protect it. She's hoping her millions of fans will take her lead and also become more aware of the problems facing the earth.

Perhaps most importantly for Kylie, she is on top of the pressures that come with living your life under the media's harsh glare.

Although Kylie is always sure to look her professional best, in past years she has occasionally been tired and felt low, trying to cope with her meteoric rise to fame and loss of privacy.

These days she accepts all the ups and downs of her profession and gets on with doing the very best she can.

"I've reached the stage now where I don't care what people say. I used to get offended and take it very personally, but now I've got enough belief in myself to think 'to hell with them. I'll do what I like'!" she laughs.

"People have sometimes said I'm manipulated. I'm 'produced' like everyone else in the music industry and to some extent my image is overblown. But I haven't lost sight of the real Kylie and I'm certainly not manufactured. I decide what clothes I wear, what songs I sing, who I go out with and what to do with my money."

E NINETIES

Kylie spent 1989 making "The Delinquents" (May 1 – June 23) and immediately after recorded her second album "Enjoy Yourself". Kylie had been the biggest selling artist in the UK in 1988 with the first "Kylie" album, so expectations were high for record number two.

"Enjoy Yourself" lived up to every expectation – and more.

Kylie was much happier with the album, feeling she had progressed considerably as a singer and covered a far wider range of musical styles. It was a more mature album, without losing the special qualities that had made "Kylie" so successful.

Kylie was keen to get out and take the album to her fans via concerts, which she did in Japan and in the UK with the 'Hitman Roadshow' in October.

Record producer Pete Waterman, who organised the tour, has always been full of praise for Kylie, but after the tour, he had this to say:

"She's a star. She has the potential to become an enormous celebrity. The sky's the limit for what she could achieve. She could be the biggest female singer of all time, if she wants to.

"Kylie has a very special talent. She just comes alive the moment she's put in front of a camera or a microphone. I've seen her look ill with exhaustion after flying in from Australia, step straight on the stage and be electric. It's the sign of true star quality."

"I do look back on the early photos and cringe. I've usually got green smudges around my eyes and my flick hair-do and I think 'aagh'. In those days you just had a make-up artist and you didn't really know how you should look, whereas now if I don't like something, I say so."

After the British tour, Kylie's schedule continued to be hectic. On October 29 she appeared at the Smash Hits Readers' Poll night with friend Jason Donovan. They received a sensational welcome from the 8000 fans, especially when they eyed Kylie in a gold spangled bra and pink hotpants!

Kylie was awarded the Best Female Solo Singer and Most Fanciable Female Singer and sang "Never Too Late".

Two days later came a major turning point in Kylie's career. She made her final on-screen performance as Charlene in "Neighbours". It was 18 months after her departure in Australia, and as much as Kylie loved every minute of her time in Ramsay Street, it was time to leave Charlene behind.

Like many actors, Kylie always has a good laugh whenever she thinks back to her early appearances on "Neighbours".

On November 25 Kylie was honoured in her homeland when she joined other Aussie music greats like INXS with her own 'Star Of Fame' outside Sydney's Hard Rock Cafe. It was an unusually cool day but hundreds of fans waited patiently for Kylie to arrive and leave her mark in the wet cement.

"It's nearly as big as me," Kylie laughed to the fans, "but that isn't too difficult".

Next, Kylie made a quick dash back to England for the "Delinquents" premiere and to turn on the Regent Street Christmas lights.

The traditional Christmas lights ceremony began in 1954 and is usually carried out by a member of the Royal family. In past years Joan Collins and Dame Edna Everage have also had the honoured task.

Tens of thousands of young fans carrying 'We love you' placards waited two hours in very cold weather for Kylie to arrive in Regent Street. People stretched out ½km in either direction, giving police a tough time keeping on-lookers behind the barricades.

Kylie, wearing a glittering black jacket with zebra striped leggings, told the shivering crowd:

"I'm honoured to be following in the steps of royalty and Dame Edna - well, she's the closest thing Australia has to a queen."

Four days later the streets of London again came to a standstill for the world premiere of "The Delinquents". Fans crowded Leicester Square to watch the stars arrive and gave a massive cheer when Kylie appeared, looking radiant.

While in London, Kylie was quick to give her support to Live Aid 2, a project again inspired by Bob Geldof for famine relief in Africa.

Kylie joined Jason, Bros and other recording stars in a Stock, Aitken and Waterman produced version of "Do They Know It's Christmas", which rocketed up the charts.

Next came the Australian premiere of "The Delinquents" on December 20. Kylie was determined to do something extra special for her hometown fans - and boy did she have a surprise in store.

K Y L I E

"People often ask how I can stay down to earth. I think it is just common sense on my part. My family are really down to earth and supportive. They'd be just as happy if I was working in a typing pool or in computers," she says.

"Mum and Dad don't get caught up in anything but they do have to suffer in their own way. I think I've got the best parents anybody could possibly have. I really mean that."

Carol and Ron Minogue really do have their hands full because their other daughter, Kylie's sister Dannii, has a successful career of her own.

Dannii was singing and dancing in a children's variety show called "Young Talent Time" long before Kylie had started acting. Dannii released her first single "Love And Kisses" and a debut album this year and is also one of the stars of Australia's other top-rating soapie "Home And Away".

Fans almost didn't recognise her! Kylie appeared in a short, cropped platinum wig. Her outfit was equally as dazzling – a brilliant, super-short sequinned mini with a naughts and crosses pattern. Bright green shoes and naughts and crosses earrings completed her stunning look.

Kylie arrived on the arm of boyfriend Michael Hutchence in a battered old '50s Dodge. It was a star-studded night with 600 of the top celebrities in Australia partying-on till the early hours.

Critics on both sides of the world raved about Kylie's performance as Lola Lovell and "The Delinquents" was a huge box office hit, too.

After such a hectic couple of months Kylie had a well-earned break with her family in Melbourne at Christmas. The Minogues are a very close family, and despite Kylie's busy schedule, they always make time to be together.

And that's one reason why Kylie thinks she's been able to sustain her career.

"I suppose a lot of people would imagine that I'm jealous of Kylie but I'm honestly just thrilled for her," Dannii says.

"She obviously was what a lot of people were looking for at the time and she realises that. It hasn't made her big-headed or conceited in any way.

"She has had to toughen up. She's changed from being an innocent into someone who can cope with showbusiness at its worst. The real proof of Kylie's ability is that people like her music and keep watching her on TV and film."

Bravo, Dannii! Maybe now those silly rumours about the sisters disliking each other will finally be dismissed.

Kylie kicked off the new decade with her first, and long-awaited, concert tour of Australia. During January she buried herself in rehearsals with her funky eight-piece band, a male vocal group and her four great dancers.

This time the tour was 'all-live' and would be a full 90 minute show. Tickets of course sold out quickly. Everyone from Kylie's teenage fans to trendy fashion-setters were keen to see what Kylie could come up with.

The February tour was simply a sensation. Even the toughest critics were forced to agree Kylie could sing and dance with the very best performers in the world. She proved to be a dynamo on stage, always entertaining and warm, yet spot-on in the toughest and most energetic dance routines.

The tour was such an overwhelming success, it continued on to the UK and Europe in April and May. Kylie was enjoying herself so much, she didn't want to stop!

Everywhere Kylie travelled she was besieged by fans – at concerts, outside hotels and in even stranger places:

"I was in the airport lounge one time in the toilets. I heard this bustle outside the toilet and I knew it was the cleaner. She was waiting there till I got out! Then they ask you to sign something and say 'Have you got a pen?'

" 'Well, no I don't. I'm just going to the toilet.' The strangest things like that happen to me all the time."

Kylie loves performing on stage, but she's the first to admit the other side to touring is not nearly so enjoyable.

"It can get lonely because you go out and you may be making all these thousands of people happy and then you get back to your hotel room and you're completely on your own.

"It's like 'what am I going to do now? Who can I call?' It's usually too late to go out and because of the time difference, it's often hard to call home.

"So you can be pretty lonely and that's where a support group is necessary. It sounds like therapy, but there's my manager, my assistant and friends, who are especially important. Friends who understand what I do. It's great if one of my girlfriends or my Mum or Dannii can travel with me. I really enjoy that."

By mid-year, Kylie had turned her attention to America. With "Enjoy Yourself" released there, Kylie spent several weeks doing promotion. She was also keen to talk to producers about her next film project.

There has been no shortage of offers since "The Delinquents" but Kylie is very careful she makes the right career moves. She sees no reason why she can't juggle singing and acting careers.

"I love them both. To me, singing and acting complement each other. They can be done alternatively or combined in the form of a musical. When doing music videos for example, acting is very helpful.

"In both areas, I would like to learn more and continue to develop. Knowing that some things only come with time, I'm willing to progress gradually and try not to rush too fast and end up falling over!

"I would like to think I could continue combining both, but who knows? I might veer one way or the other. Currently I'm alternating between the two. It also depends what offers there are in the future, people's tastes change and they are volatile industries."

As one of the most popular stars in the world, Kylie has every reason to look forward to the future – whatever it brings. One thing's for sure, she's not ready to retire yet!

"I always think I can do better. I'm my own worst critic. I believe that there's still so much for me to achieve."

By mid-1989, Kylie had achieved a career full of highlights in just a few short years, but there was still one area she had yet to tackle – live concert performances.

ON TOUR

With her new "Enjoy Yourself" album due for release in October, and feeling more confident than ever, Kylie decided the time was right.

She also had a point to prove. She was keen to answer critics who said she couldn't perform outside a Stock, Aitken, Waterman studio.

Kylie decided to start her concerts in Japan, a country where she has had staggering success. "I Should Be So Lucky" was number one for 12 weeks in Japan and was the biggest selling single. In March 1989 Kylie had five singles in the Top 40, including the number one, three and four! Kylie has visited Japan many times for promotion but this time she was keen to have a better look outside the big cities. And guess who she had as a travelling partner? Her mum, Carol.

"Kylie and I have very few opportunities to spend time together so I have to make myself available and travel with her when I can," Carol says.

Kylie and Carol spent a few days holidaying at the Hakone National Park, a beautiful place on the east of Fuji-Yama, with lakes, hot springs, forest and peace and quiet. Just what Kylie needed to prepare for the big shows.

The tour was called "Disco in Dreams" and also featured Sinitta and Dead Or Alive.

The first show was in Nagoya, Japan's third largest city, 30 kms from Tokyo. Next was Osaka and then the climax of the tour for 40,000 fans in Tokyo in a concert dubbed "The Biggest Disco In History". The enormous hall had thousands of lights and lasers and everybody dancing and having a ball – Kylie too!

"It was really fantastic. It was great to give myself totally to my public. The crowd was very receptive, especially in Osaka, where the stage was close to the audience," Kylie says.

"I was a little nervous before going on in Tokyo but I said to myself 'let's do it and forget there are so many people out there'."

The tour was so successful a one-hour television special was produced called "Kylie On The Go", with Kylie as Executive Producer. The special showed Kylie and the tour party rehearsing, sightseeing, performing and trying out Japanese culture.

Another highlight Kylie will no doubt remember was a visit to the Osaka concert by Michael Hutchence. The Australian pop star and lead singer of INXS, lives in nearby Hong Kong and decided to drop in – and boy, was he impressed.

"I'm amazed at her performances. I didn't really know what to expect but what I saw was just unbelievable. She has so much energy, she is just terrific. It was definitely worth the trip."

Next came the eagerly-awaited tour of Britain. Kylie was to be the star of the Hitman Roadshow tour, with all tickets free, given away by radio stations.

Kylie was more than a little nervous, but plunged into gruelling rehersals with her four dancers Venol John, Richard Allen, Paul Smith and Kevan Allen. The tour began on October 15 at London's Hammersmith Palais. Nine dates from Bristol to Birmingham followed and the result was unanimous. Kylie was a sensation!

Kylie started the shows with the first song she ever recorded, "The Locomotion" and then performed several hits from her albums "Kylie" and "Enjoy Yourself."

She dazzled fans with spectacular costumes, appearing on stage in a stylish white, trouser suit, but in a move that brought the house down, she stripped that off to reveal skimpy, red hot pants and a glittering bra! Charlene was never like this!

Capacity crowds waved Kylie scarves, stomped, clapped and cheered to a deafening roar. 3000 fans crammed into the Edinburgh Playhouse, prompting one Edinburgh paper to write 'Kylie-mania swept through Scotland like a gale force storm!'

At Manchester's Apollo, two teenagers were lucky, lucky, lucky, when they ended up on stage for a dance routine with their heroine. The two girls were the envy of the 2000-strong screaming crowd when they were plucked on stage by bouncers.

Pete Waterman, one of the producers of the roadshow, had this to say about Kylie.

"We were a bit worried that with Kylie we might not get the adulation we got for Jason's tour, but by golly, we have! We're getting the same reaction... but just a bit louder. I can't think of a time, and I've been doing this since 1967, when girls have screamed at another girl like this. That's a new phenomenon."

Kylie finished the tour with the Smash Hits Reader s' Poll night on Sunday, October 29, where she performed "Never Too Late" before 8000 screaming fans. She was named Best Female Solo Singer and Most Fanciable Female. She collected the awards in a gold spangled bra and pink hotpants.

The British tour had given Kylie a taste of the excitement of performing before an audience and she was determined her Australian fans should not miss out. In November she announced there would be a full-scale concert tour of her homeland, this time with a live band and a 90-minute show.

It was a natural step on from the shorter Japanese and British tours, and with those under her belt, Kylie felt confident she could now have her own band and sing for a longer period of time.

She spent most of January preparing for the tour, assembling a band, working on choreography and checking the set design.

Her four dancers, Venol, Richard, Paul and Kevan flew to Australia. Venol even turned down a posting with the Royal Shakespeare Theatre

Company in London to join the tour. Venol masterminded the choreography for the shows, working closely with Kylie for weeks.

Kylie also enlisted the help of Stock, Aitken and Waterman's engineer Yoyo, who engineered the "Enjoy Yourself" album. He too, flew to Australia to do the sound for the tour.

"It will be a great challenge for me. Doing this tour is a risk because it's really putting myself out to be either raised up or thrown sticks at, but that's what this whole business is about," Kylie says.

"It's pretty scary putting yourself out there, but you'll never learn if you don't take the plunge."

The first concert was set for February 3 in Brisbane, the capital of the northern sunshine state, Queensland. But days before a rumour spread like wildfire through the media that a group called "The Singing Budgies" were booked to play at Melbourne's trendy Cadillac Bar on Monday, January 29.

Kylie's Australian fans know 'the singing budgie' is how the media often call her, so word soon spread and the secret warm-up gig was no longer a secret.

More than 1200 people jammed into the club for the 10 pm performance, while hundreds more crammed the street outside trying to get in!

Kylie admits she was a little apprehensive but her hometown crowd gave her a tremendous cheer when she took the stage, which no doubt helped. The band gave a spirited 18-song set, kicking off with "The Locomotion".

Many of Kylie's former "Neighbours" chums were in the crowd, along with friends and colleagues. A great night was had by all – well, except for those who couldn't get in!

After such a great start, Kylie was on her way. The "Enjoy Yourself" tour, which took in Brisbane, Sydney and Melbourne, was an overwhelming success.

The four dancers constantly thrilled audiences with their acrobatic and funky dance routines and more often than not, Kylie danced right along with them. Everyone was impressed with Kylie's sheer fitness and energy and just how good she had become as a dancer.

All the hits were there and everyone sang right along. Fashion-wise, Kylie again was a sensation. She started the shows in a slinky, black catsuit and hat, next was a spangled hot pants and top set and the show ended with shorts and a jacket in the design of the Australian flag.

The last show in hometown Melbourne was especially important to Kylie. She was thrilled to have her family in the audience and worked even harder than ever.

Overall, the tour left no doubt that Kylie is very serious about her musical career and is ready to spread her wings and take on the future.

She enjoyed the tour so much, she immediately queried her manager about the possibility of taking the all-live show to England. Although she had enjoyed the Hitman Roadshow tour, Kylie was keen to mount the full-scale concert for her English fans.

Plans were quickly made and in March it was announced Kylie would perform in the UK, and Europe, in April and May. Tickets sold out all over the country, hours after box offices opened.

Once again Adrian Scott was Kylie's musical director – in fact Kylie decided to take an all Australian band with her on the English and European shows.

It was only six months after the Hitman Roadshow, but fans and critics alike could clearly see the giant steps Kylie had taken. Little Charlene had been left well behind – Kylie Minogue had truly made her mark as an accomplished performer.

Rock on, Kylie!

The media have written many stories about the magical qualities that make Kylie's records so special and so successful.

IN THE STUDIO

Her famous hit-making producers Stock, Aitken and Waterman don't give many interviews and few people are allowed inside their studios. Kylie first visited the PWL (Pete Waterman Limited) studios in late 1987 to record "I Should Be So Lucky".

One person who remembers that first trip by the 18-year-old Kylie, and who has worked on all her records since, is sound engineer Yoyo.

"I remember her doing "I Should Be So Lucky". My first impression of Kylie was that she was very shy. I didn't work on that record because I was doing something else, but I remember when it was being mixed, hearing the chorus and one verse.

"I woke up the next morning and I was singing that song, so I knew it would be a hit."

Yoyo, 22, has worked at PWL for four years. His unusual nickname came at primary school when friends could not pronounce his real name Boyoya Olugbo. Yoyo was born in the UK to Nigerian parents.

After finishing school, he bought a keyboard and, remembering lessons he had as a child on the piano, began playing again. He decided he wanted to work in the music industry and enrolled for a couple of production courses.

"After that I went around to every studio in London asking for a job as a tape operator. I wanted to get the ideas and learn how to record properly.

"PWL had been opened about six months and I got a job there as the tea boy. I got everyone's food, made the tea, did odd jobs – you don't actually do anything but sort of hang around."

When Yoyo started, PWL was a small operation with maybe a dozen people in the studio and five office girls. But once the hits started for Bananarama, Rick Astley, Mel and Kim, Sam Fox and Kylie and Jason, the company had an enormous expansion.

"I couldn't tell you how many people work there now. It's in two buildings. I pass people all the time that I didn't know worked there," he laughs.

Yoyo engineered Kylie's last album "Enjoy Yourself" and has been the sound engineer on her concert tours of the UK, Japan and Australia.

"Kylie's improved a hell of a lot during the past year or so. I've seen that. Vocally she's a lot stronger, and more confident. It all boils down to experience.

"I think the last album is a lot more mature. Kylie wants to take more of a role in the production side of things now. She wants to learn that side of it. You get experience and more involvement as you go along, so it will be interesting to see what the future holds."

Yoyo lists "Tell Tale Signs", "Never Too Late" and "Hand On Your Heart" as his favourite Kylie songs. He was thrilled to be asked to do Kylie's sound at her concerts and had a great time in Australia .

"It's great to be able to work with Stock, Aitken and Waterman and actually see the process from the very beginning, from the writing of the song all the way through the recording.

"Thousands of people would love to be in their shoes."

Kylie gets asked hundreds of questions every week from media all around the world, but it's not often that Kylie gets asked to talk about the one thing she loves most – her music.

ME AND MY MUSIC

Sure, she gets asked about her hit producers Stock, Aitken and Waterman but usually journalists want to know about romance, how much money Kylie's made or other topics.

"It's funny. I've made two albums and I've toured, but no-one ever wants to talk about music."

It's time to set the record straight.

When Kylie was growing up, she was a 'disco child'. She remembers the first record she ever bought as being a compilation of disco songs. She loved to grab a hair brush, pretending it was a microphone, and dance around the lounge-room singing along to her favourite songs.

Kylie occasionally listened to her parents' records, like The Beatles or The Rolling Stones, too.

Kylie says her first major influence was seeing the film "Grease" with John Travolta and Olivia Newton-John. Kylie's mum took the three Minogue children to see the film, but it was Kylie who was most affected.

She particularly loved the 'Greased Lightning' dance, which was the rock'n'roll theme of the 50s film.

"It inspired me a lot. After seeing the film, I dreamt I could be like Olivia Newton-John – an Australian actress and singer who had made it internationally.

"I thought she was fantastic. I was about ten years old at the time."

Next came the Abba phase.

The Swedish group comprised of two men and two women, had staggering success in Australia in the mid to late 70s. Kylie again imitated one of the girls – the blonde one Agnetha – and with her friends often staged 'dress-up' concerts at home.

Kylie can't remember the first live concert she ever saw, but one of the earliest was Boy George in 1984.

Ask Kylie what is the best concert she has ever seen and the reply is instant – Prince's Lovesexy tour in London in early 1989. Kylie is a big fan of Prince and has been since "Purple Rain" days.

"I am a die-hard Prince fan although it certainly doesn't show in my music. He's a really interesting person and the only artist who I really admire as a fan. He's so outrageous and different.

"I used to scream at the film "Purple Rain". I must have seen it countless times. I think his music is really innovative."

Kylie also likes the Motown acts, such as The Four Tops, Marvin Gaye and Stevie Wonder but there is no one particular artist that Kylie has been influenced by.

"I think I try to take from everyone I see rather than have one particular influence. As far as female singers go, I admire Madonna a lot. I think she is one woman who has taken control of her career.

"She's opened up the way for Debbie Gibson, myself and all the other young female singers who are in the charts these days.

"She's diversified into theatre and films. It just shows that you can start as a pop singer and go on to do a lot more, and I respect her for that."

At the moment, Kylie is right into Young MC, a black American rapper.

Although like Madonna, Kylie is keen to diversify, she wants to keep her acting and music careers separate, which is why she has only one song on "The Delinquents" soundtrack, "Tears On My Pillow".

" I wanted to keep the film as an acting piece. I like the fact that my song is not distracting during the movie, it just runs over the credits."

Some media have been quick to report that Kylie and her sister Dannii are planning to record a duet – but that's not true, not yet anyway.

"We've written a couple of songs. In a way, it's just messing around and having fun together but if anything came out of it, that would be great.

"Contrary to what many people write, we're really interested in each other and what each other does".

When Kylie released her first album in July 1988, many critics were quick to say she was 'just another Stock, Aitken, Waterman' act, 'a flash in the pan' and that despite the staggering sales around the world, Kylie's career would never last.

ENJOY YOURSELF

With her second album "Enjoy Yourself", Kylie had something to prove. She was determined to show she was serious – very serious – about her music.

The result speaks for itself.

"Enjoy Yourself" debuted at number two on the UK charts, hitting the top spot the following week. Within six weeks of release, the album had sold more than one million copies in the UK alone.

The success of "Enjoy Yourself" was even more heartening to Kylie considering she had faced the daunting task of following-up the phenomenal "Kylie" album.

Every performer will tell you the pressures and expectations of topping a successful record are enormous. There's the dilemma of keeping to the style that fans have grown to love, while at the same time allowing the artist to mature.

In Kylie's case, she was nearly 18 months older when she recorded "Enjoy Yourself" and she wanted that to show.

"I know my music probably means nothing to somebody experiencing a midlife crisis, but people shouldn't dismiss something just because it is not relevant to their own lives.

"Kids come up to me and say 'wow, at last somebody who understands my problems'. That for me justifies the sort of songs I sing."

To Kylie, a song shouldn't be judged on how profound or high-minded its themes are. She says: "Alright, so my music is not political, it's not heavy. It's just fun. Is there anything wrong with fun?"

Well said, Kylie!

"Enjoy Yourself" includes the singles "Hand On Your Heart", "Wouldn't Change A Thing", "Never Too Late" and "Tears On My Pillow", all rocketing to the top of the charts.

Several of the tracks have special meaning for Kylie lyrically, too.

"'Heaven and Earth' runs parallel with my views on the environment and what I, along with everybody else, can do to help conserve and protect it. As I may be in a position to influence some people, I feel the song has a valid message.

"I don't want to preach to anyone, and I don't think the song does. It conveys the simple but important message that no-one can change the world overnight, but if we all put a little effort towards caring for our environment, we can keep this beautiful place, which we all too often take for granted, for future generations."

Kylie is also fond of "Wouldn't Change A Thing", which had a vibrant film-clip to promote it. It was the first Kylie video to be shot outside Australia – but the costumes were Australian!

"The song says that even if no-one else in the whole world can understand what you see in someone... who cares? It's what you believe that

The resulting album is more mature and more ambitious than her debut. It has more diversity and touches on everything from soul to 1940s big band tunes. The songs showcase how Kylie's vocals and her confidence sparkles off the record.

With more experience under her belt, she felt confident she could play a greater part in shaping the record and so this time had more input into the production process. It's a practice she definitely wants to continue in the future.

Kylie is adamant her music – pop music – has a valid place in today's music industry, even if some high-brow journalists think to the contrary.

"I sing pop songs aimed at kids, with subjects like the girl with the crush on the guy at the end of the road who doesn't know she exists. That sort of thing is important when you're 14," she says.

really matters... you shouldn't have to change a thing for anyone. It is good to have confidence in what you're doing and trust in your own judgement."

Another lyric Kylie particularly likes is "Never Too Late."

"It follows my philosophy to always try to look at the better side of things. Don't give up hope if you firmly believe that something can work out. And remember that good things come with time. It's also saying that it is OK to forgive, after all, we all make mistakes."

Choosing a name for an album is always difficult, but in "Enjoy Yourself", Kylie has a title everyone can appreciate! She also chose it as the name of her concert tour.

"It is not an unusual message for a song, but sometimes we forget to do the obvious... enjoy ourselves! With so many pressures in our society, we have to remember to look after ourselves, be happy, and make the most of what we have."

Kylie is now gearing up for the recording of album number three. It is a few months away yet, but already she is thinking about where Kylie Minogue the singer, is to go next.

There's no doubt Kylie's fashion sense and personal style has played a major part in her success. And, in the past year, Kylie has simply been a knock-out!

KYLIE STYLE

Older, more confident and more relaxed, Kylie has taken bold steps in the fashion stakes, making headlines and magazine covers all over the world.

She received the ultimate compliment in British fashion in August last year, when she joined the list of the world's most beautiful women on the cover of the prestigious Tatler magazine. Only one other singer, Transvision Vamp's Wendy James, has won the Tatler cover.

Although she picks up clothes wherever she is travelling, Kylie has remained loyal to Australian designers, wearing Down Under creations whenever possible.

FOLLOW ME

JANUARY 80 $4.80

Bimbo
OR
BRAIN?
Kylie Minogue bites
the bullet

PARTY
Clothes
that pose

GREEN MURDER
One of the most criminal
land scams of all time

FATAL OBSESSION
The tragic life of Perth's
Princess

KYLIE

She usually enlists the help of Sydney stylist Nicole Bonython, a partnership that began in early 1988, when the pair met at a fashion shoot. Nicole's husband Grant Matthews is one of Kylie's favourite photographers.

"Nicole's great. She sends me different things and keeps me up with what's happening. Like she rang me up and said 'Kylie, I've got some great fringed pants for you'. I thought 'My god, I don't want to look like a hippy!' But she sent them over and I loved them."

Kylie particularly likes the designs of avant-garde couple Peter Morrissey and Leona Edmiston, who work from a small shop in Sydney's Strand Arcade. Kylie has sequinned tops, lurex outfits, slinky bras and mini-skirts from the couple's collection.

Australia's leading contemporary designer Ian McMaugh came up with tight, beaded dresses, pearl bustiers and satin and sequinned clothes for the Japanese tour.

For all the designers, it's a chance to make their mark on the world's fashion stakes, thanks to Kylie.

STYLE

The newest member of the Kylie fashion team is Yvonne Savage, who did hair and make-up on "The Delinquents".Kylie liked Yvonne's work and personality so much she hired her as a personal assistant. Yvonne has now worked on all Kylie's tours, helping her look her best on stage.

Another valuable member of Kylie's team is British make-up artist Charlie Green. Like so many of the people Kylie works with, Charlie has become a good personal friend.

But although she has a great team behind her, Kylie still loves to go shopping herself.

"I have the best excuse in the world because you can't be seen in the same things, you know. One must go shopping!" And when she does, Kylie has a keen eye for what she likes.

"I probably couldn't put it into words but I know what my style is and when I see something, I can say 'yeah, that's definitely me'. Normally I'm just in jeans and a t-shirt, but sometimes it's really good to get dressed up and go over the top."

THE DELINQUENTS

One of the highlights of the past year for Kylie was the release of her first film, "The Delinquents".

After shooting in Australia between May 1 and June 23 1989, Kylie was on tenter-hooks awaiting the reaction to the film's Christmas release.

Back then, she said:

"It is pretty nerve-wracking waiting because some people will be ready to criticise but I have to be strong. I am proud of the film, I really am. I think it's fantastic and I have to stick to that.

"If people hate it and it's a flop – well, that's all there is to it. But I have to believe what I believe and not listen to what other people say."

Kylie's concerns, of course, never eventuated. Australian and UK critics praised the film and particularly Kylie's performance as Lola Lovell. In both countries "The Delinquents" broke box office records in its first weeks of release.

Kylie was also quick to dismiss claims that the film was unsuitable for teenagers.

"'The Delinquents' is about kids and it's about growing up. And yes, it's about sex and running

away and abortion but they are real and you can't hide kids from that."

Kylie's commitment to the film was matched by her enjoyment in doing it – she loved every minute of it!

"I was completely insecure for the first week because I knew the crew and other actors would have preconceived ideas about 'a prima dona Kylie Minogue' and what I would be like. But I worked hard and really looked inside myself for new emotions.

"The film will always be a very special memory to me."

Kylie became good friends with "The Delinquents" crew and enjoyed the close, family-like relationship of the seven-week shoot.

"I remember one night when we'd all been working really hard and had been under a fair bit of pressure, we decided to go to the local disco in Maryborough, where we were filming.

"You can imagine what the local disco is like in a very small country town like Maryborough, but anyway we all went and had a really great night.

"We all danced our heads off until almost morning! There were early calls on the set the next morning but it was one of those nights where we all let our hair down and had a ball."

Maryborough was besieged with the world's paparazzi all trying to get a glimpse of Kylie for a world exclusive. But where once this would have upset her, now Kylie laughs it off.

"We turned it into a game, trying to spot the photographers hiding all over the place. They were up trees or in a building nearby. It was really good fun.

"I mean, I can't stop any of that. You can't get rid of them but I know how to stand up for myself now."

The Maryborough residents became very protective of 'their' movie and joined in the game letting the production know whenever a photographer tried to buy his way into one of their houses overlooking a film location.

Another interesting story from the film concerns the house that Lola and Brownie decided to live in. Production designer Laurence Eastwood designed the house, which was built at the studios.

It was an authentic Queensland house of the 1950s with verandahs and all structural timber. It was a real house – all it needed was a roof, stumps, electricity, plumbing and a block of land to put it on.

When filming was completed, everyone was reluctant to see such a nice house destroyed, so the production team arranged for it to be sold through the local paper. It was eventually bought by the Warner Village Roadshow Studios.

One of Kylie's happiest memories is working with her American co-star Charlie Schlatter. A worldwide search had gone on for months to find a 'James Dean style character', until Charlie was signed.

He celebrated his 23rd birthday on the first day of filming – a great way to start work!

Charlie had previously appeared in the films "18 Again", "Heartbreak Hotel" and with Michael J. Fox in "Bright Lights Big City". And guess what? Charlie had never even heard of Charlene or Ramsay Street!

"It's true. Once I got to Australia I realised what a

huge star Kylie is there and in England. I guess I'm the envy of every guy in the world playing her lover!"

Charlie's enthusiasm, charm and sense of humour quickly endeared him to "The Delinquents" team. He tried to teach the crew how to play American football and was always full of energy.

"Charlie reminded me a lot of Craig McLachlan, who played Henry in 'Neighbours'. Charlie was just the life of the set. He was very loud and very American and always playing around. We had a great time."

Charlie is quick to return the compliment about his famous leading lady.

"Kylie's fantastic. Not only is she a terrific person, she's also a great actress – in fact, the best I've ever worked with. We've become firm friends and I'm sure we'll keep in touch with each other, both on a personal and professional level."

The friendship between Kylie and Charlie certainly helped them in the film's more intimate love scenes – scenes that caused the film's TV commercials to be banned in the UK and toned down in Australia because the authorities deemed them to be too raunchy. But Kylie says the fuss was all over nothing.

"Lola is very passionate and the film is the story of their love, so of course there are going to be love scenes. But you just catch a glimpse of virtually nothing. It's all really tasteful. I wouldn't have let it through if it wasn't."

Kylie admits she and Charlie were nervous shooting the love scenes, the first for both of them.

"It was pretty funny because (director) Chris Thomson sat us down – it was like a parent talk before we did it. He was very understanding. We had a closed set, although I was never naked.

"At one stage Charlie had nothing on but by then we knew each other pretty well, so it was okay.

"If I'd read an interview before with an actor talking about a love scene saying 'It's just another day's work', I'd be going 'Oh, come on, there's got to be something', but there's not.

"Honestly, it's just a tougher day's work."

Charlie is now starring in a new American TV series, a remake of "The Pink Panther", which combines animated characters with actors like "Who Framed Roger Rabbit?"

Both Kylie and Charlie are thrilled with their performances in "The Delinquents", and the critics seem to agree.

For the final word on the film, here's some comments from the two men who made it happen:

"Kylie is an extraordinary actress. I knew she was going to be good when we first started rehearsing, but I honestly didn't know she was going to be this good. I didn't realise at first the strength of her determination and ambition to be an actress.

"The only time she was ever irritable was with herself, whenever she didn't get something right on the first take." (Director Chris Thomson)

"She is a consummate professional, and as well as lighting up the screen whenever she appears, she also has that indefinable quality that compels you to watch her. Whatever 'it' is – she's got it!" (Producer Alex Cutler)

Charlene walked out of Ramsay Street after 2½ years.

'Bye Charlene!' one newspaper screamed, as "Neighbours'" UK fans reached for tissues when Charlene kissed Scott for the last time and drove away.

THE ACTRESS

For Kylie Minogue, Charlene had been her apprenticeship in acting. For 2½ years, Kylie had learnt about her trade, about camera angles, lighting, scriptwriters and production schedules.

She believes it was the best beginning any young actress could have hoped for. Sometimes the schedules were very tiring, and combined with promotion, left Kylie exhausted, but working that hard, also gave her the opportunity to learn quickly.

Since leaving "Neighbours" in 1988, Kylie has devoted most of her time to her music, but all the while she is on the lookout for that special script.

It took a lot of searching to find "The Delinquents", a story she instantly fell in love with.

"It did take a while to find the right script. I was getting sent a lot of scripts from people who just wanted to have my name there to sell it at the box office.

"As an actress, I wanted something completely different to Charlene and something that would

be a challenge for me. It's important for me that I continue to grow as an actress."

Making "The Delinquents" has definitely left Kylie hooked on the medium of film.

"In film every line is important so you just don't waffle over it. You're trying to shape your character. You have to be precise," she says.

"In a series like 'Neighbours', you just talk all the time. Someone has to be coming in the back door or something has to be happening. In film, it's like two or three months so you really put everything into it for that time.

"Everyone is very dedicated. But in a series , if there's someone you don't like, you have to live with them and you can get quite angry. It gets monotonous and it can be very boring and you go stale.

"I liked the fact that in the film, the character had a beginning and an end. You could see where the character was going. But in a series, you don't know what's going to happen so it's harder, I think."

Kylie and her manager have been sifting through scripts since "The Delinquents" looking for a suitable project to tackle. And surprise, surprise, if Kylie isn't keen to make a comedy!

"I would love to do a comedy. It would be just great. I don't think I'm funny at all. I'm pretty witty

– I don't know about funny – but I'd like to do a comedy.

"It would be difficult and I'd need to have a very experienced director to guide me, but I'm really keen to do it sometime in the future."

Australian viewers had the chance to see Kylie try comedy several years ago when she appeared on the country's top-rating series, "The Comedy Company".

Kylie appeared in a couple of scenes, including one where she and Jason Donovan were in bed in pyjamas arguing! Everyone was surprised by Kylie's comic talents, so don't be surprised if you hear Kylie has signed to appear in a comedy film.

Kylie is often asked about her favourite actresses. She has several, but none that she would say were 'idols'.

She is a big fan of the veteran Katherine Hepburn, admiring her as much as a women as a fine actress. She is also fond of Deborah Winger.

"She's a very versatile actress but I like her best in 'Terms of Endearment'. It's a very emotional, tearful and touching role – exactly the sort of part I'd like to tackle."

There's no doubt "The Delinquents" saw Kylie come of age as an actress, and has many critics eating their words. Wherever she goes from here, we can be assured she will tackle it as the competent professional she's worked hard to become.

KYLIE SPEAKS OUT!

"My parents have never been pushy, she business types. They simply supported me in whatever I wanted to do. As a family, we are very close."

"In ten years, I may be married with two kids sitting at home making jam all day."

"I'm not into formal religion but I do believe there's some sort of God, though in what form I'm not sure."

"I'd love to travel around England and the Greek Isles with a backpack."

"I did it myself and nobody can deny that. It was me and I know it was me and it was bloody hard work – but that's so satisfying."

"Whatever happens to me, I'm still human. I get in bad moods. I cry. With all the interviews I do, people think they know me, but I never reveal my true inner self. That's reserved for those closest to me."

"It sounds like I'm a complete hippy, but I have found myself more. It's a sense of self and a sense of direction and, because of that, I'm really looking forward to the future."

"I do get a lot of crap most of the time from journalists. But that's fine. I can handle it."

"It's best to treat press gossip as a game, because that's what it is in a way."

"Yes, I support nuclear disarmament and I think it's good the public is becoming more aware of the subject."

"The best present I ever bought myself was a juice extractor. It might not sound like much but it's wonderful to have fresh fruit juice whenever you feel like it."

"I always wanted to have a car like Fred Flintstone with the feet poking out the bottom."

"I'm quite happy with what has happened. I consider myself lucky and I don't think that I've missed out on any childhood or anything because of it."

"Recently I had breakfast in Paris, lunch in Luxembourg, dinner in Brussels and, when I finally got to bed that night, I was in Amsterdam – and that was all in one day!"

"I have learnt to toughen up to bad press and nasty reports."

THE KYLIE TRIVIA QUIZ

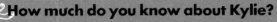

How much do you know about Kylie?

1. Which Kylie single plays over the credits of "The Delinquents"?

2. What occupation does Kylie's younger brother Brendan have?

3. Kylie won this nickname when she accidentally punched Jason on the "Neighbours" set.

4. Who wrote "The Delinquents" novel and who is she related to?

5. What is Kylie's highest selling solo single world-wide?

6. Kylie had a part-time job at school, doing what?

7. Who is Kylie's favourite male singing star?

8. Before "Neighbours", Kylie and Jason appeared together as children in another Australian series, set around an airport. What was it?

9. In which video-clip did Kylie wear the same dress in three different colours?

10. What star sign is Kylie?

11. Name the song and the artist of the music that played when Scott and Charlene got married?

12. What is Kylie's favourite car?

13. Which Australian actress played Lola's mother in "The Delinquents"?

14. What's the name of Kylie's family dog?

15. What was Charlene's occupation in "Neighbours"?

16. Although she sticks to a healthy diet, there is one sweet food Kylie loves. What is it?

17. What TV series does Kylie's sister Dannii star in?

18. Kylie's mother Carol came from which country?

19. Which vegetable does Kylie hate the most?

20. What is the occupation of Kylie's father Ron?

ANSWERS:
1. Tears on my Pillow. 2. Cameraman. 3. Bruiser. 4. Cirena Rohan, the Aunt of Aussie tennis champ Pat Cash. 5. I Should Be So Lucky. 6. Working in a video-shop. 7. Prince. 8. Skyways. 9. Hand On Your Heart. 10. Gemini. 11. Suddenly by Angry Anderson. 12. 1957 Thunderbird. 13. Angela Punch McGregor. 14. Gabby. 15. Motor-mechanic. 16. Chocolate. 17. Home And Away. 18. Wales. 19. Brussel sprouts. 20. Accountant.

WHEN Kylie hit the spotlight around the world, she was just 18 years old, not long out of school and living with her parents.

KYLIE - PERSONALLY

During the past four years she has travelled down a sometimes rocky road, living her life in public and growing up in front of the media and her fans.

At times it hasn't been easy and it is a mark of Kylie's determination that she has come through it all with her feet firmly on the ground and with her happy-go-lucky personality intact.

Now she's at the ripe old age of 22, she feels on top of the world.

"It sounds like I'm a complete hippy but I have found myself more," she says. "It's a sense of self and a sense of direction and, because of that, I'm really looking forward to the future.

"For a while there I was like 'Oh, what's around the corner. I wish I could have a break'. But now I've got new enthusiasm and I'm really keen to be working. I want to make the most of what I am."

Over the years, Kylie has tried to make her gruelling work schedule as relaxed as she possibly can. She did try yoga classes to help unwind, but

with her commitments found it impossible to keep at it.

Kylie is fond of visiting health resorts every so often for a pep-me-up. This had led newspapers to report 'Kylie is close to a nervous breakdown' or 'Kylie is anorexic' but this is just not so.

After weeks of travelling and promotion, what better way to get over tiredness and jet lag than to give yourself over to healthy eating, massages, fun exercises and some peace and quiet! Kylie has several places in the UK and Australia she likes to visit to help recharge her batteries.

She also likes to travel with an essential oils burner. In fact it's almost the first thing she packs! The burner lets off a lovely, relaxing perfumed smell giving antiseptic hotel rooms a soothing new atmosphere.

Kylie has also been working out with exercises several times a week. With all the strenuous dance routines on her recent tour, she says there's no way she could have made it through the concert, and still been able to sing, unless she was in top shape.

Kylie is also taking more interest in the world around her. Like many people, she is concerned with the destruction of the environment and has been doing her best to learn more about the problems, and the possible solutions.

Kylie has been reading literature from the Australian Conservation Foundation for the past year or so. So committed is she to helping the group, she donated the proceeds from the Sydney premiere of "The Delinquents" to it.

She has also been investigating the possibility of having all her record sleeves made from recycled paper. This would be a great innovation in the music industry.

Kylie would also like her fans to be more aware of the environment. Below, she has listed five simple suggestions everyone can follow. Let's all help to keep our world healthy.

1 Don't buy or use aerosol cans containing fluorocarbons. These contribute to the depletion of the ozone layer.

2 What goes down your drain? Don't throw oil, tea leaves or fat down the kitchen sink. You may end up swimming with them at the beach.

3 Recycle. Start a compost heap for food wastes. Recycle glass and paper. Your local council can tell you where.

4 Try to buy products that are 'environmentally friendly', everything from washing powders to kitchen cleaners.

5 Tell your friends to get in on the act, too. Everybody can do something to help, no matter how small.

THE KYLIE FAN CLUB

The addresses to write to are:

Australia and New Zealand

Private Bag 5, Albert Park 3206, Melbourne, Australia

Rest of the World

P.O. Box 292, Watford, Hertfordshire, England WD2 4ND

WRITTEN BY: Chrissie Camp
DESIGNED BY: Gravity Design Pty Ltd
PHOTOGRAPHERS: Simon Fowler, Paul Cox, Bob King, George Vernon, Isabel Snyder, Rod Stewart, Peter Mac.
MANAGEMENT: Terry Blamey Management Pty Ltd